Fun to Learn
All about
ANIMALS

Illustrated by
Dave Burroughs

Designed and produced by
Autumn Publishing Ltd
Chichester, West Sussex

Printed in Spain

ISBN 1 85997 594 1

BYEWAY
B O O K S

CONTENTS

INTRODUCTION

Our world, planet Earth, was formed millions of years ago. Since the beginning of time, and long before humans walked this planet, Earth has been home to millions of creatures.

The thin skin of solid rock around the outside of the Earth, called the crust, is made up of pieces called plates. There are seven main plates and several smaller ones. The main plates form the seven continents of the world: Europe, North America, South America, Africa, Asia, Australasia and Antarctica. Even the most remote parts of our planet are home to many different animals. The scorching hot deserts of Africa, the tropical rainforests of South America and the freezing ice sheets of Antarctica are all home to a great range of animal life.

In *All About Animals* you will discover some of the amazing creatures that share the planet with us. You will read about their homes, their habits, what they eat and how they look after their young. The colour illustrations will show you what each animal looks like and how they have adapted to their natural environment. There is a chapter for each continent. The chapter called the Polar Regions includes the continent of Antarctica in the South Pole as well as the Arctic region in the North Pole. You can read how these two frozen extremes are home to some fascinating animals.

Earth is a relatively small and fragile planet. Many of the animals in this book are now rarely seen in the wild. The major change affecting these animals is the huge and ever-increasing number of humans on the planet. This change is causing great damage. As more and more people demand more and more land, the habitats of wild animals are becoming gradually smaller and fewer. We are forcing plants and animals to exist in even smaller areas.

The destruction of these natural habitats means that many species are threatened with extinction. Some of them will disappear forever; many of them already have. Poachers and hunters are still killing animals despite laws to protect them, and we continue to pollute the air, soil, rivers and oceans.

But there is hope for the future. People are becoming more aware of these problems and realise that we must share the Earth with other animals. We must all appreciate the need to stop the damage, save our planet and plan for a brighter future.

MAP OF THE WORLD
The seven continents

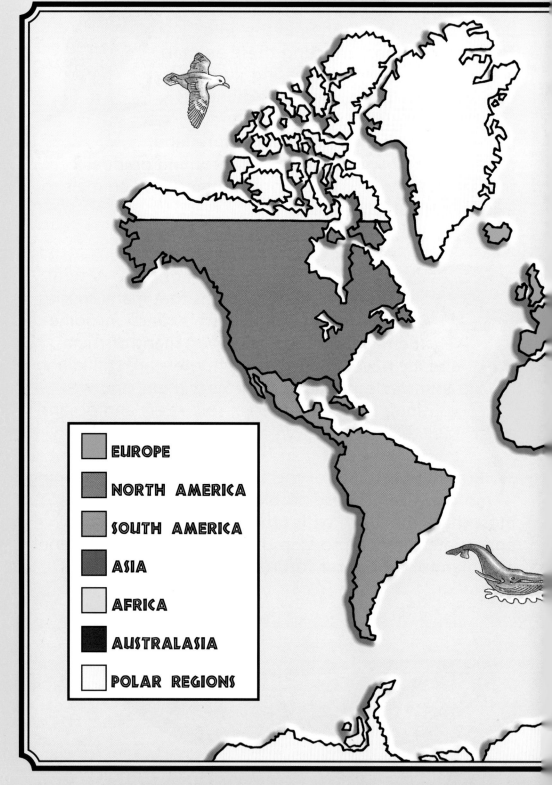

EUROPE

NORTH AMERICA

SOUTH AMERICA

ASIA

AFRICA

AUSTRALASIA

POLAR REGIONS

BADGER

It is easy to recognise the badger by its black and white striped face. This **nocturnal** animal spends most of the day underground in a burrow, called a **set**. The badger is very good at digging. It uses its powerful legs and strong claws to clear away soil to make a home. The badger is a sociable animal that lives in groups.

Badgers often travel long distances in search of food and use the same paths over and over again. They will eat almost anything from small **mammals** to **insects**, earthworms and frogs. Badgers also enjoy eating roots, plants and fruits. They have poor eyesight and use their sense of smell and hearing to find food.

The badger's underground set consists of many tunnels.
In the living areas they use dry grass and leaves for bedding.
Badger cubs are born underground and spend the first few
weeks of life in a special nursery area.

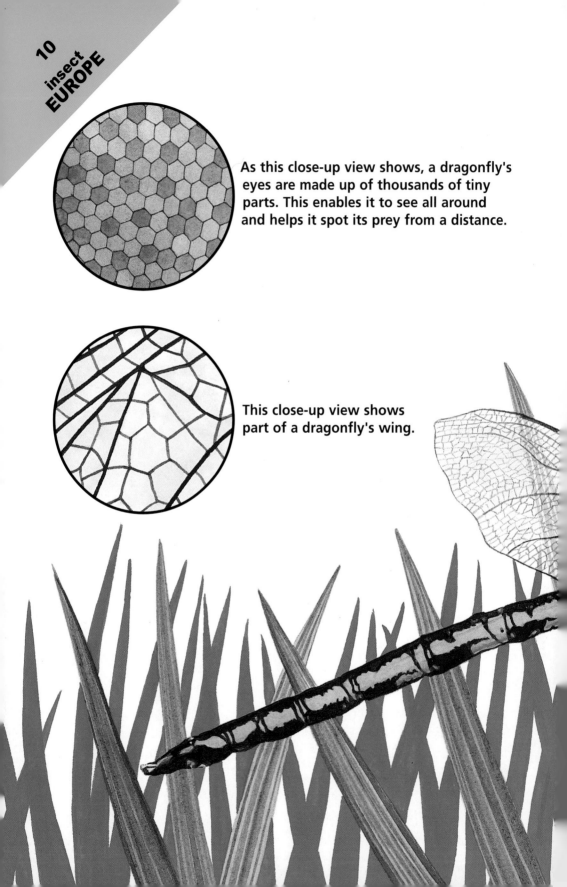

As this close-up view shows, a dragonfly's eyes are made up of thousands of tiny parts. This enables it to see all around and helps it spot its prey from a distance.

This close-up view shows part of a dragonfly's wing.

EMPEROR DRAGONFLY

The emperor dragonfly can often be spotted near ponds, rivers and canals during warm summer months. It is one of the fastest of all flying **insects**. The male emperor dragonfly is a beautiful bright blue whilst the female is green and brown.

Emperor dragonflies spend most of their life underwater. They will only emerge to fly for a few weeks in order to lay their eggs. They usually fly a few metres above water and will occasionally land to rest on reeds or in trees. Emperor dragonflies catch most of their **prey** whilst they are in the air.

GREY SEAL

The grey seal's thick layer of fat, called **blubber**, helps it to survive in freezing-cold waters. It spends a lot of time hunting in the sea. Large eyes enable it to see in murky waters, but hearing and taste are more important for this animal when hunting. The seal's powerful fins and smooth shape mean it can swim very fast. A grey seal can stay underwater for up to 20 minutes at a time, but will usually come up for air after about ten minutes.

Although grey seals generally hunt on their own, they form groups on the shore where they rest and dry out. A rocky island or a quiet cave also make a perfect resting spot. During the breeding season, the remote beaches become crowded as females give birth to their pups and males establish their **territory**.

The seal's muzzle and whiskers are very sensitive. They enable the seal to sense movement in water made by its prey.

Females give birth to a single pup. Pups are born with a creamy white coat that will start to turn grey after about three weeks.

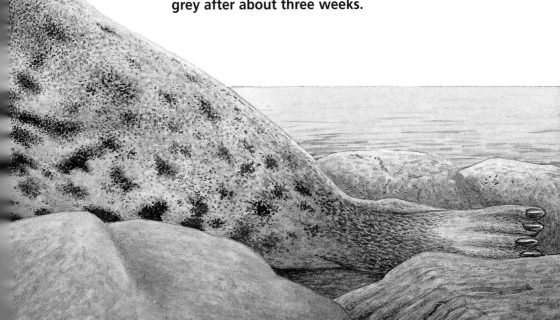

When a hedgehog senses danger it rolls up into a tight ball to protect itself.

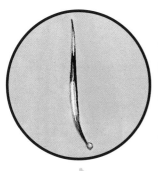

There are around 3000 spines on a hedgehog's back. Each spine will last for about a year before it drops out and a new one grows in its place.

HEDGEHOG

Being a **nocturnal** creature, the hedgehog is generally active at night and spends most of the day asleep under hedges and bushes. Its prickly spines are a good defence against attack from other animals.

Hedgehogs live in a variety of **habitats**, and are usually seen near woodland, parks, playing fields and gardens. They hunt at night for earthworms and **insects**. They have been known to eat food put out for cats and dogs in urban gardens!

Like many other small **mammals**, the hedgehog survives the winter months by **hibernating**. It will eat as much as it can during the autumn, then build a thick nest in which to spend the winter. Favourite nesting places include stacks of wood, compost heaps and haystacks.

OTTER

The otter is a shy and solitary animal. It lives on the banks of rivers and lakes or near the seashore. The otter spends most of its time in water but may spend part of the day playing on land. Its fur is short, thick and oily. When it goes ashore after a swim, water runs off its coat so that the otter's skin does not get wet.

Otters love to eat fish, and eels are a favourite meal. Otters catch fish by chasing them underwater and sometimes cornering them in a clump of weeds. Once they have caught their **prey**, otters carry the food back to dry land to eat.

Females give birth to two or three baby otter cubs in an underground burrow, called a **holt**. When a cub is about three months old, its mother will teach it to swim.

As the otter dives, its ears and nostrils close, but its eyes stay open so that it can see its prey. The otter grips its catch with sharp teeth and powerful jaws.

The tawny owl sits on a perch, waiting for its prey. The soft feathers under its wings allow it to glide down silently upon its next meal.

The tawny owl uses its sharp talons to grip the branches of trees and to grab its prey.

TAWNY OWL

The tawny owl is **nocturnal**, so you are more likely to hear its hooting **call** than to actually see the bird. It lives mainly in woodland and farmland, but can also be found in parks and cities.

The tawny owl hunts at night. Its excellent hearing means it can locate **prey** in complete darkness. Using sound, the owl slowly turns its head to detect the position of the prey before swooping down and catching it with sharp **talons**. The owl uses its sharp beak to tear up the food.

Owls eat lots of different food, depending on where they live. Those living in woodland areas tend to eat small **rodents**, worms and beetles. Nearer towns and cities, owls will eat small birds and have been known to take fish from garden ponds.

The female tawny owl lays between two and five eggs. She sits on the eggs one at a time, which means that they hatch at intervals. Once they have hatched, the female sits on the chicks whilst the male brings food.

BEAVER

The beaver lives near water in quiet wooded areas. With its large, strong front teeth, the beaver can fell trees by gnawing through the trunks. The beaver then uses the branches and trees to make dams across fast-flowing streams. A calm, flooded area is created behind these dams. It is here that the beaver builds its home, called a **lodge**. The beaver digs the mud with its front feet and creates canals along which it can push floating logs and branches for new dams.

Beavers strip the bark off trees with their front teeth and eat it. During the autumn months, beavers spend a lot of time felling trees and gnawing them into logs. These are stored for the winter months ahead.

Beavers have large, flat tails which help them to swim fast and steer through water. Beavers warn each other of danger by slapping their tails on the surface of the water.

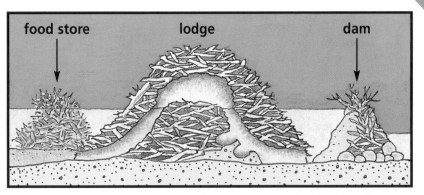

food store   lodge   dam

The area behind the beaver's dam becomes flooded with water. The beaver builds his lodge behind the dam. Underwater entrance tunnels lead to the living area. Branches stored nearby provide a winter food supply.

The beaver's large, webbed back feet are ideal for swimming.

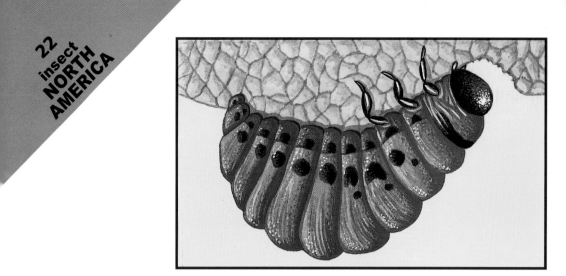

Each larva changes from a deep pink colour with black spots to a bright yellow adult with black stripes.

COLORADO BEETLE

This beetle was first discovered in Colorado, in the USA, around 200 years ago. Since then, the Colorado beetle has spread to almost every part of the world where potato crops grow.

Using its powerful jaws, this beetle and its young, called **larvae**, feed on the leaves of the potato plant. A female beetle can lay up to 2500 eggs, which hatch after a few days. The larvae start eating straight away, and in a short space of time these **insects** can strip a plant of its leaves. The beetles do not eat potatoes, as they grow underground. However, once the plant has lost its leaves the potato will stop growing. It is not long before a whole crop is destroyed.

The Colorado beetle is considered to be a **pest**. Strong chemicals, called **pesticides**, have been used in attempts to destroy it. So far, these have been unsuccessful and the Colorado beetle continues to thrive.

GRIZZLY BEAR

The most fierce and aggressive of all bears, the grizzly leads an almost solitary life in the mountains and forests of North America.

Grizzly bears spend the spring and summer resting, sleeping and looking for food. They eat fruits and berries as well as meat. In autumn they will eat a lot of food to last through their winter sleep. Grizzly bears do not actually **hibernate**, but fall into a deep sleep. On sunny days they may wake up and go in search of food. Some bears sleep in caves, but grizzly bears usually dig their own shelters in steep mountain slopes.

In its natural home, the grizzly bear has no **predators**. However, humans continue to hunt them and destroy forest areas where they live, leaving fewer of these animals surviving. They are now considered to be an **endangered** species.

Grizzly bear cubs are born blind, toothless and with very little hair. After a few months, when the cubs are old enough to leave the den, their mother teaches them to hunt for food. Bears that live near rivers soon become very good at catching fish - particularly salmon.

Bears' paws are wide and flat with long claws. A single blow from one of these powerful paws can kill an animal.

Females lay between three and seven white eggs. Males and females help to feed the black, featherless chicks that hatch after about 18 days.

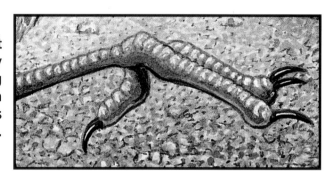

The roadrunner's feet and legs are very strong. When running at full speed, they can take about 12 steps every second.

ROADRUNNER

The roadrunner can run faster than any other bird that
flies. Although able to fly, the roadrunner prefers to stay on
the ground where it can run at very high speeds.
This bird relies on speed to escape from danger and to catch
fast-moving **prey**. Using its tail as a rudder, the roadrunner
is able to change direction quickly and easily. It runs with its
long neck stretched out and uses its tail and wings for balance.

Roadrunners live in areas that are hot and dry during the day,
but where temperatures can drop very low at night. Because of
these changes in temperature, roadrunners have a special
patch behind their wings. This patch quickly absorbs heat from
the sun and helps to
warm the bird after
a cold night.

SALMON

The salmon has a long and hazardous life-cycle. The young fish hatch and develop in the cool, clear, fresh waters of rivers. As they get older, **shoals** of salmon move downstream towards the ocean. As the salmon get used to salt water, their skin develops a silky sheen.

Some years later, the adult salmon return to the river where they were hatched, so that the females can lay their eggs. Exactly how salmon find their way back is a mystery. These **migrating** fish have to travel upstream. They leap high out of the water, over rapids and up waterfalls. Many salmon will die on the journey. Those that do survive are very weak, and few find their way back to the ocean after **spawning**.

A big salmon is able to leap up to three metres in its attempts to get above river rapids and waterfalls.

Each baby salmon, or larva, stays attached to a yolk sac that it feeds from for about a month.

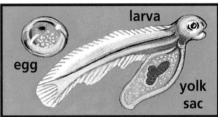

egg | larva | yolk sac

Baby skunks start to explore outside
the den when they are quite young.
They will stay in their family unit
for the first winter.

SKUNK

The striking black and white **coat** of the skunk acts as a warning to other animals. If a skunk is attacked, it will turn its back, lift its tail into the air and spray a foul-smelling liquid into its attacker's face. The liquid is so powerful that it can leave the attacker blinded for some time, but its main purpose is to allow the skunk time to escape. Because of its terrible smell, the skunk fears few other animals, including humans.

Skunks spend most of the day in a den, which they sometimes share with other animals. At dusk, skunks come out of the den in search of food. They use their long front claws to dig in the soil for grubs, earthworms, roots and fallen fruit. Although skunks do not actually **hibernate**, they will rest and sleep in their dens during winter months.

ANACONDA

The biggest snake in the world, the anaconda lives in the tropical Amazonian rainforests. The many streams, rivers and swamps provide the perfect **habitat** for this giant snake that is more at home in water than on land.

Anacondas can grow up to ten metres in length. They are fast swimmers and can stay underwater for ten minutes at a time. They lie beneath the surface waiting for **prey**, such as deer, wild pigs and large **rodents**. Anacondas usually hunt at night and spend the day basking in shallow waters.

The future of this **reptile** is threatened by the continued destruction of rainforests, and from hunters who kill it for its skin.

The anaconda lies in the shallow waters of a forest stream, waiting to grab its prey and drag it into the water. The anaconda kills by coiling itself around its prey and squeezing until the victim cannot breathe.

Some types of armadillo, like the one in this picture,
can curl up into a tight ball to protect their soft belly.

GIANT ARMADILLO

The armadillo is a strange-looking **mammal**, related to anteaters and sloths. Its body is covered with a hard protective shell that makes the armadillo a difficult **prey** for even the most determined **predator**.

The largest of all the armadillos, the giant armadillo can grow to more than one metre in length. These creatures avoid the daytime heat by resting in a burrow and emerge at night to feed. Giant armadillos use the large claws on their front feet to dig for **insects**. Their diet includes termites, ants, worms and snakes. Despite their size, giant armadillos are quite agile and can balance on their back legs with their front feet off the ground.

The giant armadillo relies on its armoured shell for defence. If threatened, it may scurry away through thick bushes or dig a hole to hide in.

IGUANA

The iguana can often be seen lying on the branch of a tree, near a river, in a tropical rainforest. It is very good at climbing and can leap from branch to branch. The iguana is also an excellent swimmer and uses its long tail to help it move through water. When in danger, it simply drops from a branch into a river, where it can stay underwater for several minutes.

Iguanas feed mainly on leaves, berries, fruit and other food that they find in trees. Like other **reptiles**, iguanas rely on the sun to warm their **cold-blooded** bodies.

The adult male has
a large flap of skin
under its throat and
a tall crest of spines
along its neck.

The female iguana
digs a chamber at
the end of a deep
tunnel and lays up
to 60 eggs. The
bright-green young
hatch out about
three months later.

The piranha's teeth are triangular in shape, with needle-sharp points and razor-sharp sides. It has strong muscles to move its jaw. The teeth in its lower jaw can be up to two centimetres long.

PIRANHA

The piranha is the most feared of all river fish. Although most piranhas are only about 20 centimetres long, their teeth are strong enough to chop through bone with a single bite.

Piranhas live in huge **shoals** or packs, and spend most of their time in search of food. They have an enormous appetite and tend to eat anything that gets in their way. Their excellent sense of smell helps them to find their **prey**. They usually eat fish, but will also attack birds and **mammals** that are swimming or standing at the water's edge to drink.

TARANTULA

These huge, hairy spiders are found in forests, often on the trunks of trees. The sticky hairs on the tips of their legs allow them to walk up shiny forest leaves. Some live on the ground, mainly in warm desert areas.

Most tarantulas build silk-lined burrows to live in. The female often spends her whole life inside the burrow. Using its front legs, the tarantula grabs any **prey** that comes too close to the entrance. It feeds on large **insects**, small lizards and **rodents**. The tarantula uses its long fangs to spear its victim before injecting it with poison.

Despite their scary appearance, most tarantulas are fairly shy and rarely attack humans. Some types of tarantula are collected as pets and now there are less of them living in the wild.

When the young spiderlings have hatched from the egg case, they spend the first few weeks of life in the burrow.

The toco toucan's feet have four toes: two point forwards and two point backwards. This enables them to get a firm grip on branches. Toco toucans prefer to hop, rather than fly, from branch to branch.

Although the toco toucan's bill is very large, it is hollow and very light. The toco toucan uses the tip of its bill to hold eggs, which it steals from the nests of small birds.

TOCO TOUCAN

The toco toucan is an extremely colourful bird. It has a bold black and white **plumage** and a large orange and black **bill**. The toco toucan spends most of its time in treetops and is rarely seen close to the ground.

The toco toucan generally feeds on berries, fruit and the eggs of small birds. It makes a nest in a tree hole, and may use the same nest for several years. When the chicks hatch they are blind and featherless.

Toco toucans are playful birds and are often seen jumping about in trees. They are not shy creatures and have even been known to go into houses to steal food and scare pets!

The young sloth clings tightly to its mother's fur for the first nine months of its life.

The sloth's front feet have two claws.

The sloth's back feet have three claws.

TWO-TOED SLOTH

The sloth is an unusual animal that spends most of its solitary life hanging upside-down in trees. It eats, sleeps and looks after its young whilst upside-down, only occasionally spending time on the ground. The sloth is a very slow animal and moves just one limb at a time. It relies on clever **camouflage** to protect itself from **predators**.

The two-toed sloth has two long, curved claws on its front feet and three on its back feet. These claws help it to grip the branches of trees. The sloth finds it easier to swim than to walk, and uses its front feet to push itself through water.

Sloths are **nocturnal**, so they sleep during the day. When sleeping, they place their head on their chest and look like a hanging ball of fur. They have poor eyesight and hearing, and rely on smell and touch to find leaves, shoots and fruit to eat.

AFRICAN ELEPHANT

The African elephant is the largest and most powerful land **mammal** in the world. Despite its enormous size, the elephant is very gentle and lives in peaceful family units, or herds.

Although elephant herds may travel great distances, they do not move very far from water. Elephants enjoy a daily bath. When the water is deep enough, they will completely immerse themselves. In the dry season, they suck up water in their trunks and squirt it over themselves.

Elephants are **herbivores**, so they only eat plants. Not surprisingly, they need to eat a large amount of plants to survive. The elephant's ivory tusks are long teeth that grow throughout its life. For many years, people have hunted elephants for their tusks. Even though hunting and trading in ivory is now banned, the African elephant is an **endangered** species.

A young calf will stay in its family unit for several years. A mother will defend her young by charging at intruders.

As well as to breathe and smell, the elephant uses its trunk to tear up grass or to pull branches off trees.

The giraffe uses its long tongue to grasp leaves. It then pulls its head away to tear the leaves from the tree.

Like human fingerprints, no two giraffe coat patterns are the same. The pattern allows the giraffe to blend in with its surroundings and protects it from predators.

GIRAFFE

The giraffe is the tallest land **mammal**. Its long neck enables it to eat leaves and plants that most other animals cannot reach. When a giraffe drinks, it has to bend and spread its long legs in order to lower its head to the water.

Giraffes have very good eyesight, hearing and sense of smell. They are also very fast runners. Because they are so tall, giraffes make good look-out guards. Zebras often roam with groups of giraffes for protection from **predators**, such as lions. Giraffes will kick out with their front feet if they are attacked.

Giraffes are one of the few animals that are born with horns. A calf's horns lie flat against its head when it is born, but pop up during the first week of life.

GORILLA

The gorilla is a great ape and is one of our closest living relatives. Generally, it is a peaceful animal that spends most of its time in groups, munching leaves, resting and grooming. The lead male of a group is called a silverback because of the grey hair on his back. When he feels threatened, a silverback may stand up, beat his chest with his hands, growl and then charge at the intruder.

When gorillas drink, which is not very often, they soak the fur on the back of their hand and suck off the water. Gorillas get most of the water they need from the moisture in the plants and fruit that they eat.

Each evening, gorillas build a leafy nest for the night. They make a nest by sitting on a branch and pulling in any small branches within reach.

Because of hunting and the destruction of their natural forest **habitats**, the future of the gorilla is seriously threatened.

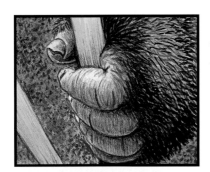

The gorilla's hands are very similar to human hands. They are good at gripping small things and are strong for climbing trees.

Although the gorilla moves on all four legs with its knuckles on the ground, most of its weight is on its powerful back feet.

Young gorillas tend to stay with their parents for about three years. A baby gorilla is carried in its mother's arms for the first few months of life.

The female Nile crocodile lays up to one hundred eggs in a hole in the sand. The sun heats the sand which keeps the eggs warm. When the baby crocodiles have hatched, the mother gently carries them in her mouth to the water.

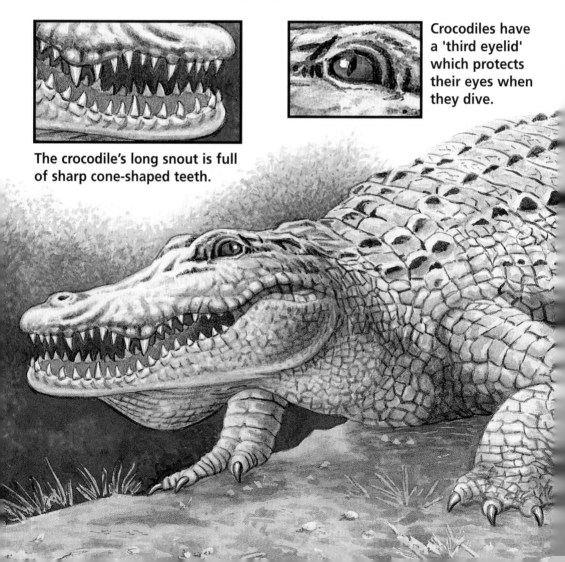

Crocodiles have a 'third eyelid' which protects their eyes when they dive.

The crocodile's long snout is full of sharp cone-shaped teeth.

NILE CROCODILE

The crocodile is a **reptile**, descended from dinosaurs of prehistoric times. The Nile crocodile is the largest crocodile in Africa and one of the largest in the world. Measuring around six metres in length, it is a fearsome **predator** which feeds on unwary animals as they drink at the water's edge. It eats **mammals**, birds, fish and even other reptiles, including crocodiles.

Nile crocodiles spend most of the day basking in the sun on the shores of lakes and river banks. They have eyes, ears and nostrils on the top of their head so that they can see, hear, smell and breathe while submerged. These crocodiles are very fast swimmers and use their long, muscular and flat tail to guide them through water.

OSTRICH

This strange-looking, flightless bird is a triple record breaker. The ostrich is the world's largest bird, and it can run faster than any other bird. It also lays the largest eggs of any living creature. With its round body, long neck and long legs, the ostrich is an impressive sight.

The ostrich feeds on plants, flowers and seeds. It lowers its long neck to peck at food. Because its head may not be visible when it is lowered in the grass, some people think the ostrich actually buries its head in the sand. While grazing, the ostrich will regularly raise its head to check for signs of danger.

These large birds used to be farmed for their soft black and white feathers, which were used to decorate clothes and hats. Today, ostriches are farmed for their meat. Ostriches have been trained to scare birds from crops and to help round up sheep.

The nest of an ostrich can contain up to 40 eggs. However, most of these eggs will not hatch. The chicks from the eggs that do hatch, join chicks from another nest. One or two adult birds guard the flock.

Unable to fly, the ostrich has developed very strong, hoof-like feet that enable it to run very fast.

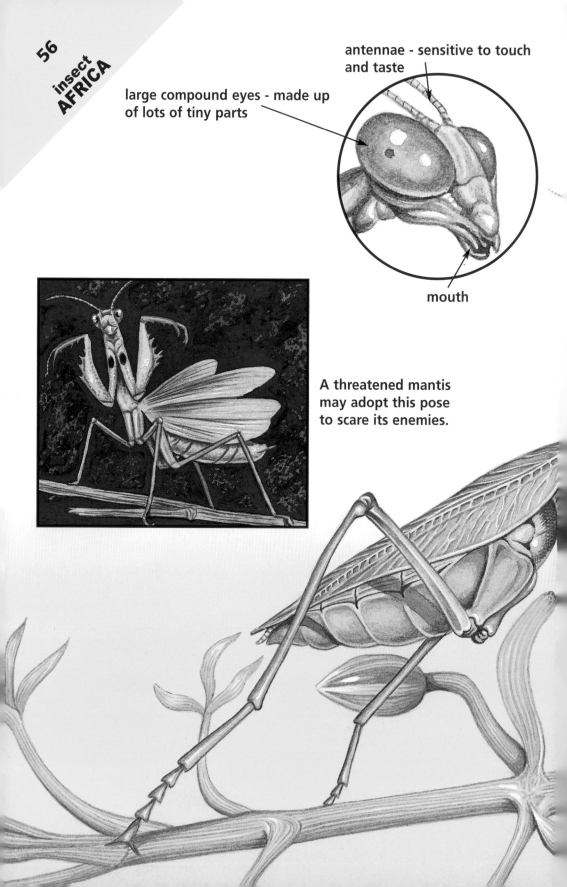

antennae - sensitive to touch and taste

large compound eyes - made up of lots of tiny parts

mouth

A threatened mantis may adopt this pose to scare its enemies.

PRAYING MANTIS

The praying mantis does not actually hunt for its **prey**. Instead, it waits for all kinds of **insects** to pass by and satisfy its huge appetite. When a likely meal comes within reach, the mantis grabs it with pincer-like front legs.

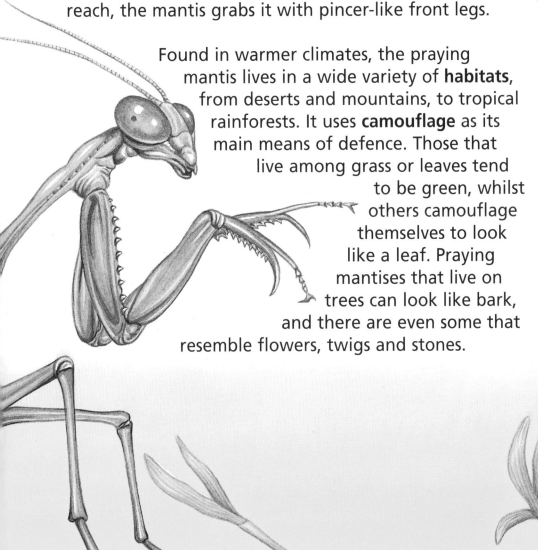

Found in warmer climates, the praying mantis lives in a wide variety of **habitats**, from deserts and mountains, to tropical rainforests. It uses **camouflage** as its main means of defence. Those that live among grass or leaves tend to be green, whilst others camouflage themselves to look like a leaf. Praying mantises that live on trees can look like bark, and there are even some that resemble flowers, twigs and stones.

BACTRIAN CAMEL

The Bactrian camel has two humps on its back. Like its cousin, the one-humped dromedary, it can go for long periods of time without water. In the heat of the desert sun, the camel is able to last ten times longer than humans without having a drink.

Camels are well-equipped for life in the desert. The soles of their feet have thick pads that expand under the animal's weight. These help to support the camel when it is walking through soft sand. Their bodies can cope with great changes in temperature. Their thick, shaggy fur keeps them warm during the night when the temperature in the desert drops. During the day, their fur stops them from heating up too quickly and losing fluid through sweating. Camels survive by eating the tough grass and shrubs that grow in these dry **habitats**.

The camel has a double row of long eyelashes above and below its eyes. These protect its eyes from dust and sand. The camel's nostrils can close in a sandstorm.

Camels do not actually store water in their humps. The humps are made of fat, which the camel can change into water if necessary.

The tiger's teeth are vital to its survival. If a tiger lost its long canine teeth, which are used for tearing meat, it would very likely starve to death.

BENGAL TIGER

Capable of killing animals over twice its size, the tiger
is one of nature's most feared **predators**. The tiger is
nocturnal, so it sleeps most of the day and hunts at night.
It is a solitary animal and does not like to share its **territory**
with other tigers. For this reason, a small number of tigers
need a large area in which to successfully hunt and live. The
tiger hunts all kinds of animals, from deer and monkeys to
wild oxen and buffalo.

The female tiger, or tigress, will give birth to between two
and four cubs. Cubs are blind for the first ten days of life.
After about six months, the mother will leave the den for
several days to hunt for food. When
they are about 11 months old the
cubs begin to hunt alone. They stay
with their mother for two to three
years before living and hunting
on their own.

CARP

The common carp, once only found in Asia, can now be found all over the world. In the wild, carp mainly live in large rivers, but they can live in most fresh water. They feed on the bottom of the riverbed, eating water snails, mussels, plants and insects. On hot afternoons, they rise to the surface to bask in the warm sunlight between the plants.

Carp have been bred for thousands of years as ornamental fish. The brilliantly-coloured koi carp were originally bred in Japan. Unlike the dull-coloured common carp, the beautiful koi may be black and red, pure white, white and red, black and white, and many other varieties of colours. They are worth a lot of money and are sometimes stolen from people's ponds.

The baby carp, called fry, tend to stay in very shallow water near the riverbank. At this stage, the young are very vulnerable to anything larger than themselves. The fry may become the prey of other fish-eating creatures, including their own parents.

GIANT PANDA

The black and white giant panda, with its round face and black 'eye patches', is one of the world's best-loved animals. It is also one of the world's shyest and rarest wild animals.

Pandas are solitary and peaceful animals that spend most of the day resting and eating bamboo. They are good at climbing and will climb the nearest tree if they sense danger. Giant pandas live in cold, damp conditions in south-western China, but their thick waterproof coat protects them. Although pandas do not **hibernate**, they shelter in caves or hollow trees during very cold weather.

The giant panda is under threat of **extinction** and is the symbol of the WWF (World Wide Fund for Nature).

The panda's diet consists almost entirely of the stems, leaves and fresh young shoots of bamboo. The panda needs to eat large amounts of bamboo in order to get enough nutrients to stay healthy.

KOMODO DRAGON

Found only on tiny islands in Indonesia, the Komodo dragon is the largest true lizard that has ever lived on land. Despite its great size, the Komodo dragon is very agile and moves quickly over the ground. It is also a good swimmer, using its long tail to propel itself through water. Like most other **reptiles**, the Komodo dragon sleeps at night. As the heat of the sun warms its blood, the Komodo dragon becomes more active and sets out in search of food.

Komodo dragons are not fussy eaters. They will eat almost anything they can catch, even other Komodo dragons. Their favourite food includes wild pigs, deer and monkeys. Adult Komodo dragons are capable of eating nearly a whole deer in one go - and will then sleep for a week to digest it!

The Komodo dragon can grow to three metres long - longer than a small car.

The Komodo dragon's thick, scaly skin is very tough and a dull grey-brown colour. This helps keep it camouflaged as it lies in wait for its prey. The Komodo dragon uses its long, thin forked tongue to 'taste' the air for food.

A female peafowl is called a peahen. The peahen does not have the brilliant colouring or magnificent tail of the peacock. Instead, her colouring enables her to blend into the undergrowth where she looks after her chicks.

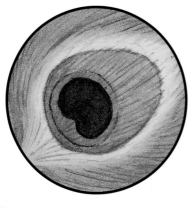

The peacock's fan is covered in beautiful, shiny 'eyes'. In its natural habitat, the peacock's feathers, or plumage, help to camouflage it against the trees.

PEACOCK

The peacock is the male bird of the peafowl and is best known for its long, flowing and colourful tail feathers. The peacock displays its tail feathers by spreading them like a magnificent fan. The feathers are decorated with beautiful patterns that look like eyes.

Peafowls live in small groups in hilly areas. They spend the day on the ground and roost in trees at night. In the wild, peafowls are threatened by tigers and leopards, and can act as an early warning system for other animals. They often become aware of big cats before other animals, and raise the alarm with a loud hoot.

DUCK-BILLED PLATYPUS

The duck-billed platypus is one of the world's strangest-looking creatures. It is about the size of a rabbit, has a soft **bill**, broad webbed feet and a flat tail. Although it is a **mammal**, it actually lays eggs like a **reptile**.

The duck-billed platypus lives near water, and nests in tunnels that it digs in river banks. It can live on land and is very good at swimming and diving. The platypus finds food in the water, where it hunts for water snails and small shellfish. Underwater, the platypus closes its eyes, ears and nostrils and uses its broad bill to sweep the riverbed for food. The flat tail acts as a powerful rudder when swimming and helps the animal to dive.

The back feet of the platypus are less powerful than the front feet, but they help to steer it through water. Each back foot has a sharp, hollow spur, which contains enough poison to kill an animal the size of a dog.

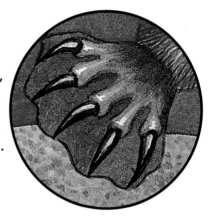

The duck-billed platypus uses its broad, webbed front feet to help it swim. It swims by 'rowing' with its front legs; pulling first on one and then the other. Its strong claws are used for digging.

In order to climb, the koala clasps the tree trunk between its front paws. Its 'thumb' and 'forefinger' spread out to give a firm grip. It then brings its back legs up together in small, quick jumps.

The toes on the back feet of the koala are also separated to help it grip the tree trunk.

Koalas cannot survive without eucalyptus leaves, and need to eat a lot of leaves every day. As they only eat certain types of eucalyptus, they sometimes have to be transported to areas where food is more plentiful.

KOALA

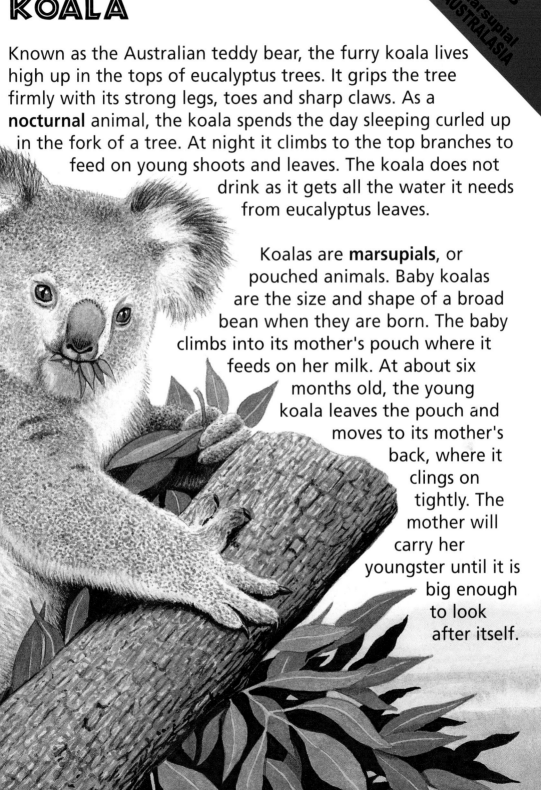

Known as the Australian teddy bear, the furry koala lives high up in the tops of eucalyptus trees. It grips the tree firmly with its strong legs, toes and sharp claws. As a **nocturnal** animal, the koala spends the day sleeping curled up in the fork of a tree. At night it climbs to the top branches to feed on young shoots and leaves. The koala does not drink as it gets all the water it needs from eucalyptus leaves.

Koalas are **marsupials**, or pouched animals. Baby koalas are the size and shape of a broad bean when they are born. The baby climbs into its mother's pouch where it feeds on her milk. At about six months old, the young koala leaves the pouch and moves to its mother's back, where it clings on tightly. The mother will carry her youngster until it is big enough to look after itself.

KOOKABURRA

The kookaburra is the world's largest kingfisher and is found only in Australia. It is often called the laughing kookaburra because of its unusual **call**.

Kookaburras hunt during the day. They look for food from their perch high in the branches of trees. Their diet includes **insects**, crabs and small **reptiles**, such as snakes. From its position in the trees, the kookaburra waits for suitable **prey** to pass beneath before swooping down to grasp it in its sharp **bill**.

Kookaburras make nests in holes, mostly in trees and sometimes in the holes of walls or buildings. The female lays two or three eggs. When the young chicks hatch, they rely on their parents to bring them food.

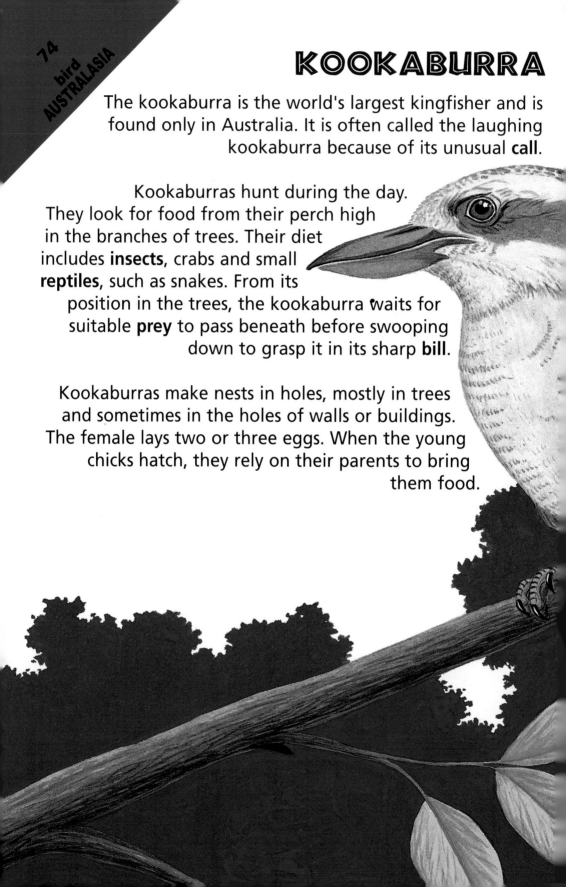

With amazing accuracy, the kookaburra swoops
to the ground to catch its prey.

When born, the baby kangaroo climbs into its mother's pouch. Once inside the pouch, the hairless joey feeds on its mother's milk. The joey first pokes its head out of the pouch when it is about five months old.

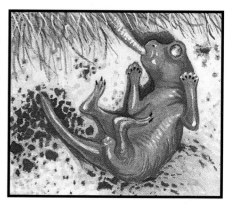

The kangaroo's powerful back legs and long feet enable it to travel at speeds of up to 65 kilometres an hour.

RED KANGAROO

The red kangaroo is the largest **marsupial**. A baby
kangaroo is called a joey. When it is born, the joey is
no bigger than a human thumb but it can grow to be taller
than a man. Despite its size, it is a **herbivore** and eats only
grass and shrubs. The kangaroo is a grazing animal that lives in
social groups. These groups are sometimes called 'mobs'.

Red kangaroos are well adapted to life in the dry, hot desert
regions of Australia. As they are mainly **nocturnal**, they rest
under the shade of a tree or scrub during the hottest part of
the day. Their powerful back legs enable them to make great
bounding leaps across the plains. Kangaroos use their long,
powerful tails for balance when they leap.

TASMANIAN DEVIL

With its thick, dark coat and short legs, the Tasmanian devil looks like a big rat. Found only on Tasmania, an island off the south coast of Australia, this **marsupial** gets its name from its rather fearsome reputation. In reality, the Tasmanian devil is a fairly shy and timid creature.

Tasmanian devils spend the day hiding in forests and woodlands. They become most active at nightfall. Tasmanian devils will eat almost anything, including **insects**, leaves and twigs. They have been known to eat rubber boots, gloves, socks and plastic objects!

Like other marsupials, the babies develop in their mother's pouch. The mother gives birth to up to four babies. Once they emerge from the pouch, the mother may carry them around on her back whilst she hunts for food. This can be a bit of a bumpy ride, and the young will often tumble off!

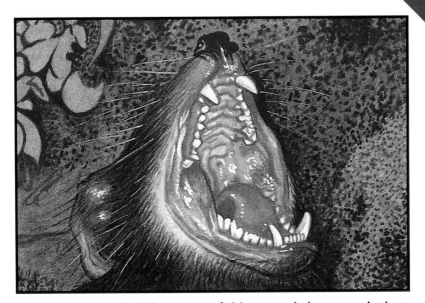

The Tasmanian devil has powerful jaws and sharp teeth that it uses for tearing meat. It will even eat fur, feathers and bones, which it can easily crunch with its strong jaws. If threatened, the Tasmanian devil gnashes its teeth together and makes loud snarling noises.

The tiger shark normally swims by moving its head in one direction and its tail in the other. The long fins at the side of its body act like wings and help lift the shark as it swims through water. Its long tail provides the power for sudden bursts of speed.

TIGER SHARK

The tiger shark is a very powerful **predator**. It will eat almost anything it can swallow. A fierce and solitary hunter, the tiger shark is armed with a set of extremely sharp teeth.

These sharks spend most of their life swimming in tropical waters, rarely stopping except to eat. Their diet includes squid, fish, smaller sharks, turtles and seals. Tiger sharks have good eyesight, but they rely on other senses to help them locate their food. Their good sense of smell enables them to pick up traces of blood in the water. They can also sense the swimming movements of other animals around them.

Baby tiger sharks are born with a full set of teeth. As soon as they are born the young sharks can hunt for themselves.

ARCTIC FOX

The Arctic fox is well equipped for life in the harsh polar climate. During the freezing winters it lives in almost constant darkness. Its bushy **coat** turns completely white, making it very difficult to see against the snowy landscape. The Arctic fox digs tunnels in the deep snow, which often become home to several family groups.

During the Arctic summer there is continual daylight and the sun occasionally warms the air to just above freezing. The fox lives in a den or burrow, which it digs in the side of a hill or the bank of a river.

Arctic foxes are **carnivores** and their **prey** includes voles, hares, birds and eggs. Those that live near the coast eat shellfish and sea urchins. If there is not much meat around, they will also eat fruit and berries. During the summer months, when there is plenty of food, the foxes hide food in their dens or push it into cracks in rocks. When winter arrives, they dig the food out of the snow.

The Arctic fox's summer coat is light brown in colour. As winter approaches, the coat will begin to thicken and change to white.

After a few weeks, cubs begin to explore outside the den with their mother. Later, the cubs learn to hunt with their parents.

The whale's broad tail propels it through the water.

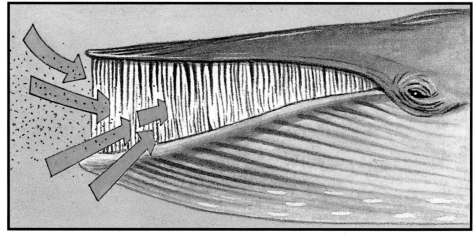

Instead of teeth the blue whale has a row of 'plates' in its mouth. These act like an enormous sieve, which collects plankton with each mouthful of water. Once it has forced the water back out, the whale licks these plates and the trapped plankton with its huge, fleshy tongue.

BLUE WHALE

Truly a giant of the ocean, the blue whale is the largest living creature. Despite its enormous size, the blue whale feeds on some of the smallest forms of life in the ocean - **plankton**. It is a surprisingly fast swimmer and catches its food mainly by diving.

Blue whales are drawn to the salty waters of the Arctic and Antarctic where there is plenty of plankton to eat. Each year the winter freeze forces the whales to **migrate** to the warm waters of the tropics. Females give birth to young whales in these warmer waters.

The future of this enormous **mammal** is still unknown. Because of its great size, it has been a target for hunters who use its **blubber** to make oils. It will take many more years of protection before this gentle giant is free from the threat of **extinction**.

EMPEROR PENGUIN

The emperor penguin is the largest seabird in the world. It is able to survive the freezing temperatures of the Antarctic ice pack and keeping warm is the main concern of this penguin. It has a thick **plumage** that traps a layer of warm air next to its skin and is kept warm by a thick layer of **blubber**. The penguins huddle in groups to keep warm.

The emperor penguin cannot fly and only waddles on land. On smooth, icy slopes a penguin may lie on its belly and 'toboggan' across the ice!

Emperor penguins feed on fish, squid and shrimps, which they chase and catch. They are very agile, graceful swimmers and are able to twist and turn quickly. They use their wings like paddles, while their feet and tail steer.

Emperor penguins do not build nests as there are very few nest-building materials to be found in the Antarctic. To protect their single egg from the cold, the penguin supports the egg on its feet and covers it with a fold of skin and feathers.

Unable to fly and not very agile on land, the penguin is most at home in water.

As soon as it is old enough, the chick will be left with other young penguins while its parents are away catching food. As summer approaches, the chick becomes increasingly able to take care of itself and will finally set out on its own.

The polar bear eats seals and seal pups. With its excellent sense of smell, the bear can sniff out a seal pup in a den up to one metre underground. The polar bear uses its big, strong paws to dig through the snow to a pup.

POLAR BEAR

The polar bear is one of the world's largest land
carnivores. This huge, strong bear has a thick white **coat**
that enables it to blend into the snowy landscape. The polar
bear also has hair on the soles of its feet to help prevent it
from slipping on the icy surface.

Polar bears live around the Arctic ice pack. They are always on
the look-out for their next meal, and seals provide their main
source of food. Polar bears catch seals by waiting at a
breathing hole or by stalking an unsuspecting seal lying on
the ice.

Polar bears are excellent at swimming and diving. They swim
using their front legs, with their back legs trailing behind.
They can dive beneath the surface of the water, with their
eyes open and nostrils
closed, for as long as
two minutes at a time.
Once out of the water,
they shake themselves to
remove the water from
their coats before
it has time to freeze.

WALRUS

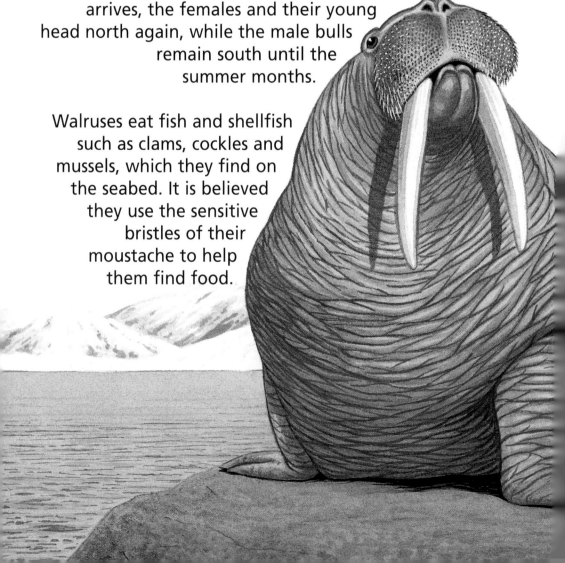

The walrus lives in the freezing Arctic. It is easy to recognise by its long tusks, wrinkly skin and bristly moustache. The walrus has very thick skin and **blubber** to protect it from the icy waters. The walrus spends its days swimming in open water, and resting on ice or rocky shores in huge numbers.

The walrus cannot survive under the ice pack when it is frozen solid. When the ice begins to thicken and spread, the walrus usually **migrates** south to warmer weather. When spring arrives, the females and their young head north again, while the male bulls remain south until the summer months.

Walruses eat fish and shellfish such as clams, cockles and mussels, which they find on the seabed. It is believed they use the sensitive bristles of their moustache to help them find food.

The tusks of the walrus are teeth that grow throughout its life. The walrus uses its tusks to get a firm grip when trying to pull itself onto the ice. The tusks are also used as weapons or simply to support its head as it rests on the ice. The tusks of a bull can grow to one metre in length.

The long, narrow wings of the wandering albatross allow it to effortlessly glide on air currents.

Parent birds feed their single fluffy, white chick for nearly nine months. When the young bird is ready to leave the nest, it sets out alone.

WANDERING ALBATROSS

The wandering albatross has the largest wingspan of any bird. The albatross may spend many months in the air, without ever touching land. It travels vast distances over the southern oceans of the world, only coming to land to breed and lay eggs.

Although it soars across the waves with amazing grace and skill, this great sea bird is very clumsy on land. Waddling along on its huge webbed feet, it often places one foot on top of the other, causing it to fall over!

The main **prey** of the wandering albatross is squid, octopus and cuttlefish. It catches them by landing on the sea and taking them from the surface with its huge **bill**.

GLOSSARY

arachnid - an animal with four pairs of legs, and usually has pincers or fangs.

bill - a bird's beak. Also the muzzle of a duck-billed platypus.

blubber - a thick layer of fat just under the skin of an animal; to keep its body warm and to insulate it in cold environments.

call - the characteristic sound of an animal.

camouflage - the natural colouring of an animal that enables it to blend in with its surroundings.

carnivore - an animal that eats other animals; usually a hunter that feeds on meat or flesh.

coat - an animal's fur or hair.

cold-blooded - an animal that cannot generate much of its own internal warmth, so its body temperature varies with the temperature of its surroundings.

endangered - a species in danger of extinction.

extinct - a species that has died out; no longer exists.

habitat - the natural environment of an animal or plant.

herbivore - an animal that eats plant food, such as shoots, stems, leaves, buds, flowers and fruit.

hibernation - a long period of inactivity or sleep that some animals adopt during winter.

holt - an otter's den.

insect - typically an animal with three pairs of legs, two pairs of wings and a body divided into three separate parts.

larva - the young of a fish or frog – between the stage of an egg and an adult.
larvae - more than one larva.

lodge - a beaver's den.

mammal - a warm-blooded animal that gives birth to babies that feed on the mother's milk. They have four limbs (they have fins if they live in water) and breathe air.

marsupial - a mammal that carries and suckles its young in a pouch; found mostly in Australasia.

migration - in nature, a journey that is usually long-distance and carried out regularly by certain animals, to find better conditions for feeding and/or breeding.

nocturnal - an animal that is most active during the night.

pest - a destructive animal, especially an insect, which attacks crops and livestock.

pesticide - a substance used for destroying insects or other organisms that harm plants or animals.

plankton - the small and microscopic organisms that drift or float in the sea and fresh water.

plumage - a bird's feathers.

predator - an animal that hunts other living animals for food.

prey - an animal that is hunted or killed by another animal.

reptile - a cold-blooded animal whose young hatch from eggs. Reptiles have lived on Earth much longer than birds or mammals - they first appeared around 300 million years ago.

rodent - a mammal with strong incisor teeth used for gnawing.

set - a badger's underground den.

shoal - a great number of fish swimming together.

snout - the nose and mouth of an animal.

spawning - the release of eggs, by a fish or frog.

talon - a claw, especially that of a bird of prey.

territory - an area defended by an animal or animals against others of the same species.